REALLY EASY PIANO

OLLY MURS

ARMY OF TWO	3
ASK ME TO STAY	6
BUSY	8
DANCE WITH ME TONIGHT	14
DEAR DARLIN'	11
HEART ON MY SLEEVE	16
HEART SKIPS A BEAT	18
HEY YOU BEAUTIFUL	21
IN CASE YOU DIDN'T KNOW	24
I NEED YOU NOW	26
LOUD & CLEAR	29
OH MY GOODNESS	32
ONE OF THESE DAYS	34
PLEASE DON'T LET ME GO	36
RIGHT PLACE RIGHT TIME	39
THINKING OF ME	42
THIS SONG IS ABOUT YOU	44
TROUBLEMAKER	46

PART OF THE MUSIC SALES GROUP
LONDON / NEW YORK / PARIS / SYDNEY / COPENHAGEN / BERLIN / MADRID / HONG KONG / TOKYO

ALSO AVAILABLE IN THE REALLY EASY PIANO SERIES...

ABBA
25 GREAT HITS. ORDER NO. AM980430

CHILDREN'S FAVOURITES
20 POPULAR HITS. ORDER NO. AM998745

CHRISTMAS
24 FESTIVE CHART HITS. ORDER NO. AM980496

CLASSICAL FAVOURITES
24 WELL-KNOWN FAVOURITES. ORDER NO. AM993366

COLDPLAY
20 SONGS FROM COLDPLAY. ORDER NO. AM989593

ELTON JOHN
24 CLASSIC SONGS. ORDER NO. AM987844

FRANK SINATRA
21 CLASSIC SONGS. ORDER NO. AM987833

GREAT FILM SONGS
22 BIG FILM HITS. ORDER NO. AM993344

GREAT SHOWSTOPPERS
20 POPULAR STAGE SONGS. ORDER NO. AM993355

JAZZ GREATS
22 JAZZ FAVOURITES. ORDER NO. AM1000857

LOVE SONGS
22 CLASSIC LOVE SONGS. ORDER NO. AM989582

MICHAEL JACKSON
19 CLASSIC HITS. ORDER NO. AM1000604

MORE 21ST CENTURY HITS
21 POPULAR HITS. ORDER NO. AM996534

MOZART
22 CLASSICAL FAVOURITES. ORDER NO. AM1000648

NEW CHART HITS
19 BIG CHART HITS. ORDER NO. AM996523

NO. 1 HITS
22 POPULAR CLASSICS. ORDER NO. AM993388

POP HITS
22 GREAT SONGS. ORDER NO. AM980408

SHOWSTOPPERS
24 STAGE HITS. ORDER NO. AM982784

TV HITS
25 POPULAR HITS. ORDER NO. AM985435

60S HITS
25 CLASSIC HITS. ORDER NO. AM985402

70S HITS
25 CLASSIC SONGS. ORDER NO. AM985413

80S HITS
25 POPULAR HITS. ORDER NO. AM985424

90S HITS
24 POPULAR HITS. ORDER NO. AM987811

50 FABULOUS SONGS
FROM POP SONGS TO CLASSICAL THEMES. ORDER NO. AM999449

50 GREAT SONGS
FROM POP SONGS TO CLASSICAL THEMES. ORDER NO. AM995643

50 HIT SONGS
FROM POP HITS TO JAZZ CLASSICS. ORDER NO. AM1000615

PIANO TUTOR
FROM FIRST STEPS TO PLAYING IN A WIDE
RANGE OF STYLES — FAST!. ORDER NO. AM996303

ALL TITLES CONTAIN BACKGROUND NOTES FOR EACH SONG PLUS
PLAYING TIPS AND HINTS.

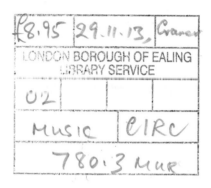

PUBLISHED BY
WISE PUBLICATIONS
14-15 BERNERS STREET, LONDON, W1T 3LJ, UK.

EXCLUSIVE DISTRIBUTORS:
MUSIC SALES LIMITED
DISTRIBUTION CENTRE, NEWMARKET ROAD, BURY ST EDMUNDS,
SUFFOLK, IP33 3YB, UK.
MUSIC SALES PTY LIMITED
UNITS 3-4, 17 WILLFOX STREET, CONDELL PARK
NSW 2200, AUSTRALIA.

ORDER NO. AM1007512
ISBN 978-1-78305-289-9
THIS BOOK © COPYRIGHT 2013 BY WISE PUBLICATIONS,
A DIVISION OF MUSIC SALES LIMITED.

UNAUTHORISED REPRODUCTION OF ANY PART OF THIS PUBLICATION BY
ANY MEANS INCLUDING PHOTOCOPYING IS AN INFRINGEMENT OF COPYRIGHT.

MUSIC ARRANGED BY FIONA BOLTON.
EDITED BY JENNI NOREY.
PRINTED IN THE EU.

YOUR GUARANTEE OF QUALITY
AS PUBLISHERS, WE STRIVE TO PRODUCE EVERY BOOK TO THE HIGHEST
COMMERCIAL STANDARDS. THE MUSIC HAS BEEN FRESHLY ENGRAVED AND
THE BOOK HAS BEEN CAREFULLY DESIGNED TO MINIMISE AWKWARD PAGE
TURNS AND TO MAKE PLAYING FROM IT A REAL PLEASURE.
PARTICULAR CARE HAS BEEN GIVEN TO SPECIFYING ACID-FREE, NEUTRAL-
SIZED PAPER MADE FROM PULPS WHICH HAVE NOT BEEN ELEMENTAL
CHLORINE BLEACHED. THIS PULP IS FROM FARMED SUSTAINABLE FORESTS
AND WAS PRODUCED WITH SPECIAL REGARD FOR THE ENVIRONMENT.
THROUGHOUT, THE PRINTING AND BINDING HAVE BEEN PLANNED TO
ENSURE A STURDY, ATTRACTIVE PUBLICATION WHICH SHOULD GIVE YEARS
OF ENJOYMENT. IF YOUR COPY FAILS TO MEET OUR HIGH STANDARDS,
PLEASE INFORM US AND WE WILL GLADLY REPLACE IT.

WWW.MUSICSALES.COM

Army Of Two

**Words & Music by Wayne Hector, Iyiola Babalola,
Darren Lewis & Olly Murs**

Olly Murs' 'Army Of Two' was written as a tribute to the *X Factor* success story's loyal fan base. To tie in with its release in February 2013, Murs launched a special Facebook application allowing his supporters to become members of the 'Olly Murs Army', by submitting their details and gaining a special membership ID and certificate. These unique IDs were later used in a fan video of the song uploaded to Murs' official YouTube channel.

Hints & Tips: Look out for E flat and B flat accidentals throughout. In bars 6–8, cross the second finger over the thumb to play the B flat.

© Copyright 2012 Salli Isaak Music Publishing Limited/Future Cut Songs Limited.
Universal Music Publishing Limited/Warner/Chappell Music Publishing Limited/Kobalt Music Publishing Limited.
All Rights Reserved. International Copyright Secured.

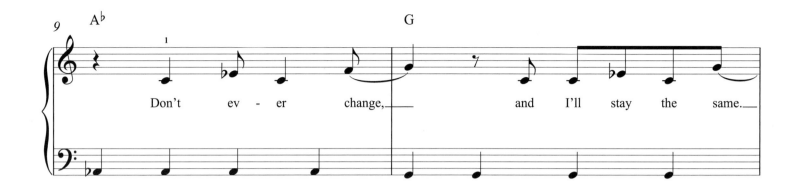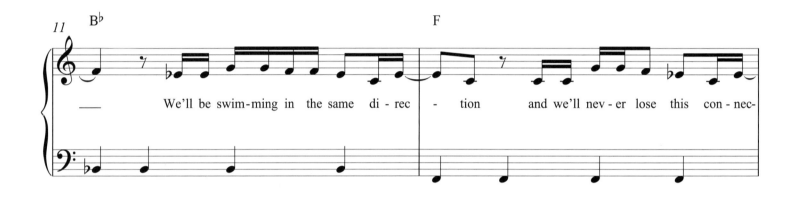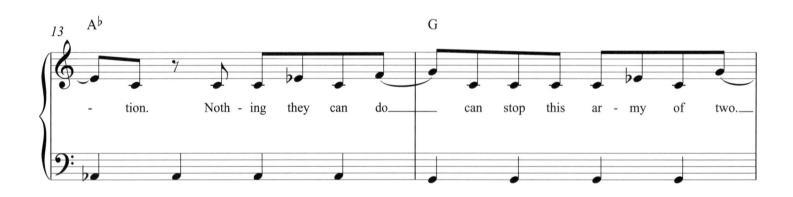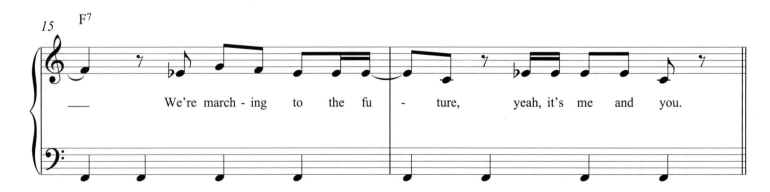

5

Ask Me To Stay

Words & Music by Christopher Braide, Christopher Difford & Oliver Murs

Having finished as runner up on the sixth series of the *X Factor*, many in the music press were sceptical of Olly Murs' ability to launch himself as an artist in his own right. However, following the release of his debut album, these misgivings were quickly countered thanks in part to the quality of the song writing on tracks such as 'Ask Me To Stay'.

Hints & Tips: The left hand is doing two things at the beginning; make sure you hold down the bottom note for the full count, while the top part moves.

© Copyright 2010 Visible Music Limited/Salli Isaak Music Publishing, Limited/BMG VM Music Limited.
Universal Music Publishing Limited/Sony/ATV Music Publishing.
All Rights Reserved. International Copyright Secured.

Busy

Words by Martin Brammer, Adam Argyle & Oliver Murs
Music by Martin Brammer & Oliver Murs

Released as the fourth single from Olly Murs' self-titled debut album, 'Busy' first rose to prominence as an instrumental version, used as a backing track for a new series of food adverts for Marks & Spencer and as the theme tune to the BBC One sitcom *Me and Mrs Jones*. Due to this added exposure, the song has become one of the most recognisable pieces of music recently released in the UK.

Hints & Tips: When you get to the chorus (bar 25) the left hand has off-beat crotchets. Don't be tempted to hold them for more than their one beat; it may help to play them slightly *staccato*.

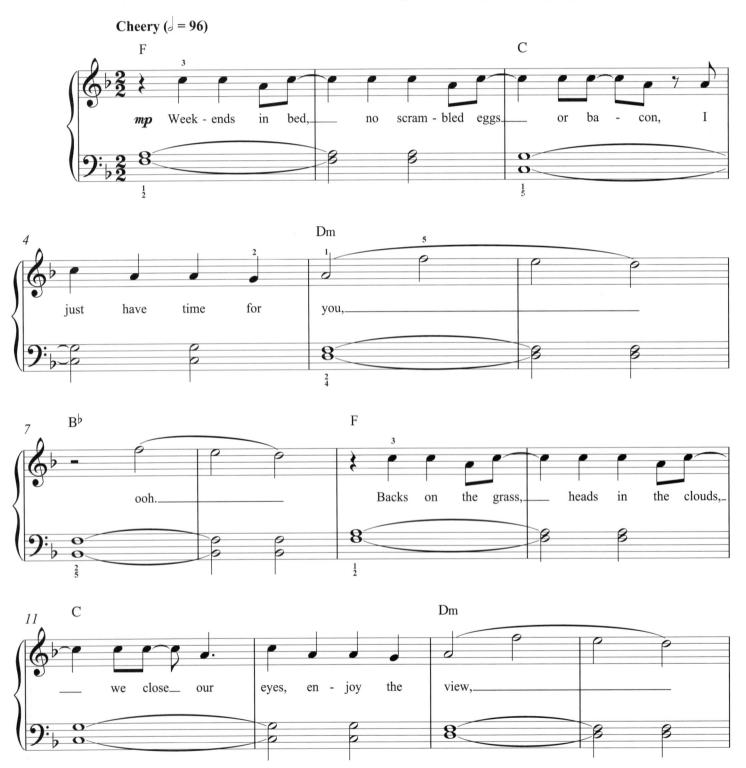

© Copyright 2010 Salli Isaak Music Publishing Limited/Peermusic (UK) Limited/Imagem London Limited.
Universal Music Publishing Limited
All Rights Reserved. International Copyright Secured.

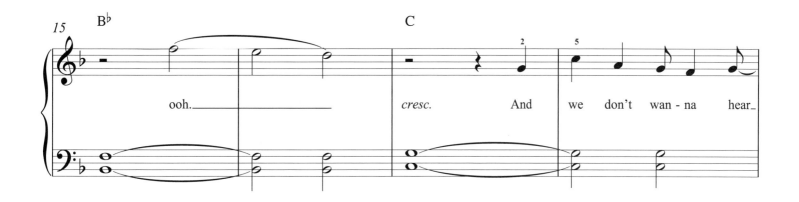

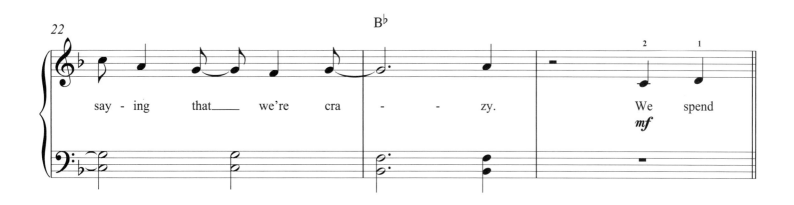
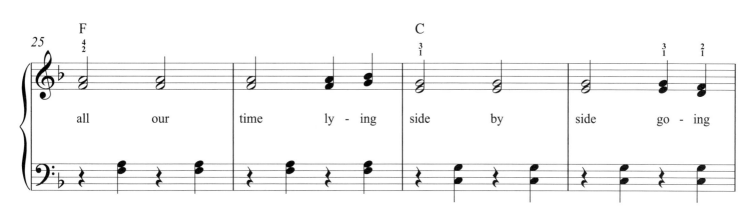

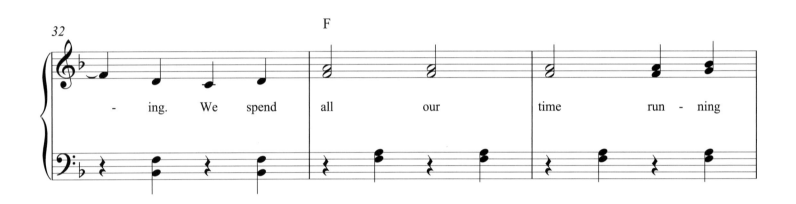
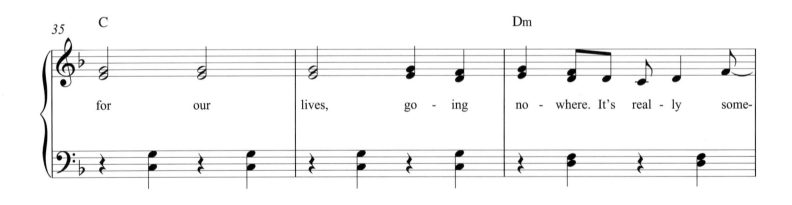
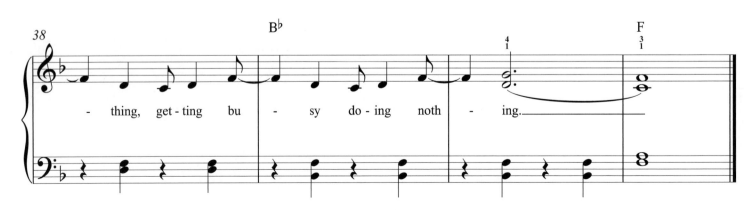

Dear Darlin'

Words & Music by James Eliot, Edward Drewett & Oliver Murs

A song about writing to someone, telling them about the feeling of loss, 'Dear Darlin'' is one of the more sombre songs in Olly Murs' repertoire. Released as the third single from his third studio album, *Right Place Right Time*, the song has been rerecorded for its French release featuring female vocals by Alizée. 'Dear Darlin'' peaked at number five on the UK chart.

Hints & Tips: The syncopated left hand rhythm is repeated a lot. Make sure you've got the hang of it before you try to fit in the right hand.

© Copyright 2012 Salli Isaak Music Publishing Limited.
Universal Music Publishing Limited/Sony/ATV Music Publishing/Warner/Chappell Music Publishing Limited.
All Rights Reserved. International Copyright Secured.

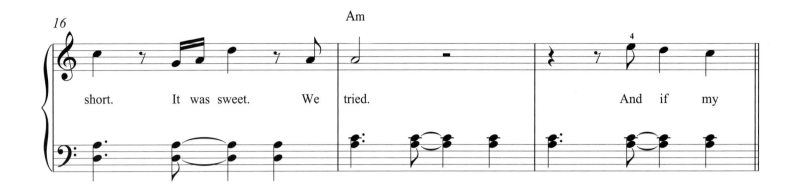
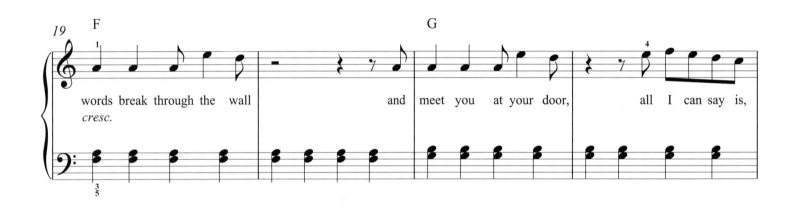
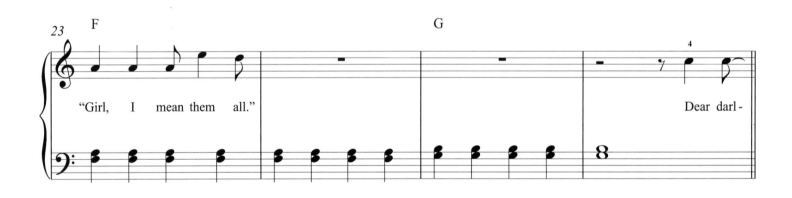

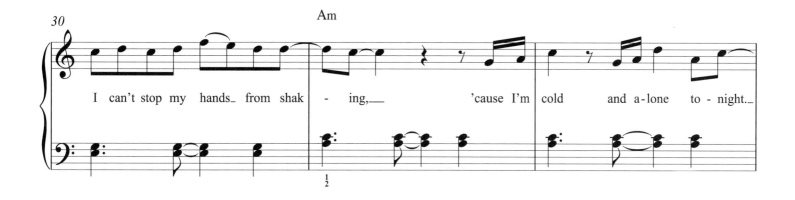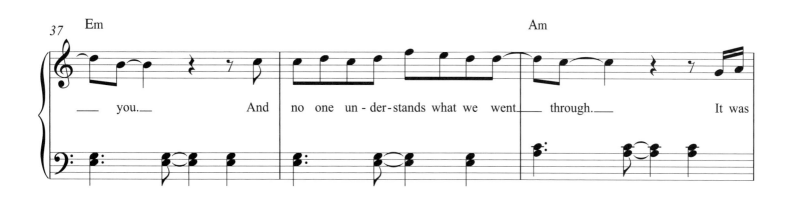

Dance With Me Tonight

Words & Music by Stephen Robson, Claude Kelly & Oliver Murs

Reminiscent of the '60s, with its hip-shaking bass line and effervescent horn section, this was the second single to be taken from the former X Factor contestant's second album *In Case You Didn't Know*. After being held up at No. 2 for a couple of weeks, it overtook the programme's 2011 charity release to become his third UK No. 1.

Hints & Tips: In this bouncy, up-beat song, remember to give the quavers that 'swing' feel. In bars 17 and 18, make sure you keep the right hand F held down while you play the notes above.

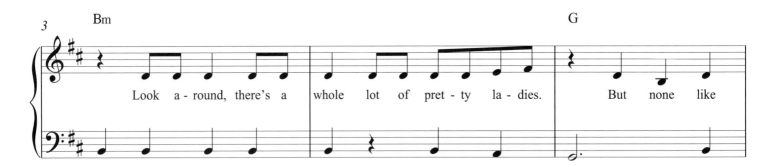

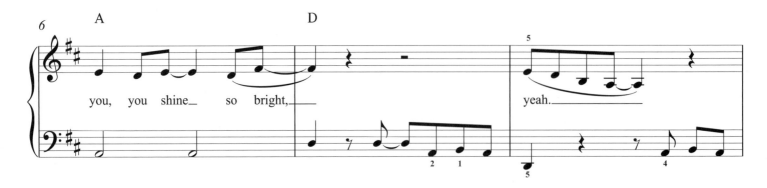

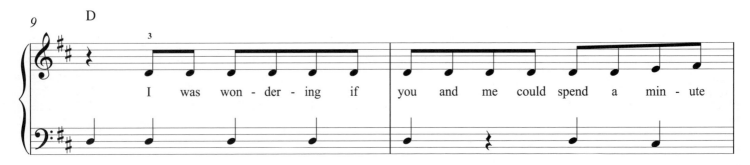

© Copyright 2011 Studio Beast Music/Salli Isaak Music Publishing Limited/Imagem CV/Warner-Tamerlane Publishing Co.
Universal Music Publishing Limited/Imagem Music /Warner/Chappell North America Limited.
All Rights Reserved. International Copyright Secured.

Heart On My Sleeve

Words & Music by James Morrison & John M Shanks

'Heart On My Sleeve' was written for Olly Murs' debut album by English recording artist James Morrison and John Shanks. A piano-based pop hit reminiscent of the modern sounds of Take That and, of course, James Morrison, Olly Murs' version of the track received strong radio play and entered the top twenty in the UK. The song was originally recorded and released by *American Idol* contestant Michael Johns for his first post-*Idol* album back in 2009.

Hints & Tips: The left hand has long, held notes in the first half. Count the right hand rhythm carefully; it often doesn't start on the first beat of the bar.

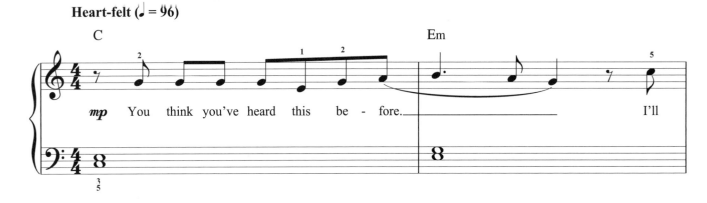

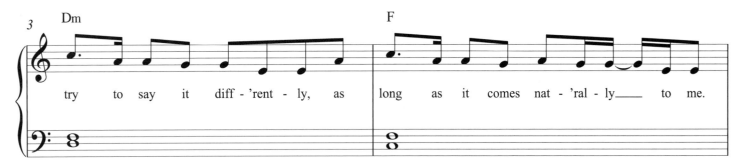

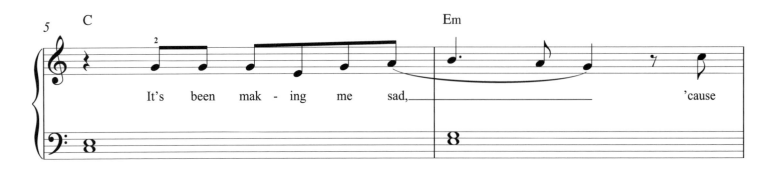

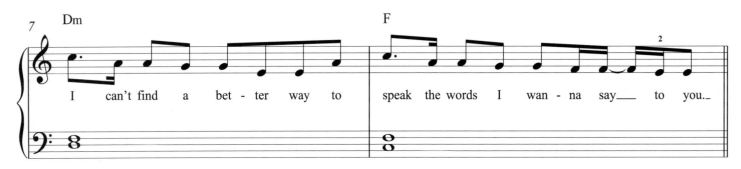

© Copyright 2011 Sony/ATV Tunes LLC/Tone Ranger Music.
Sony/ATV Music Publishing.
All Rights Reserved. International Copyright Secured.

Heart Skips A Beat

**Words & Music by Samuel Preston, James Eliot,
Alex Smith, Harley Alexander-Sule & Jordan Stephens**

'Heart Skips A Beat' features vocals from English hip hop duo Rizzle Kicks, who also co-wrote the song. Taken from Olly's second studio album *In Case You Didn't Know*, this catchy song reached No. 1 in the UK singles chart within its first week of release in August 2011. It was nominated for Best British Single at the 2012 BRIT Awards.

Hints & Tips: It is just as important to count the rests in this as it is to count the rhythms of the notes. Counting aloud might help you keep time.

© Copyright 2011 Metrophonic Music Limited/B Unique Music.
Universal Music Publishing Limited/Kobalt Music Publishing Limited/Sony/ATV Music Publishing/Stage Three Music Publishing Ltd.
All Rights Reserved. International Copyright Secured.

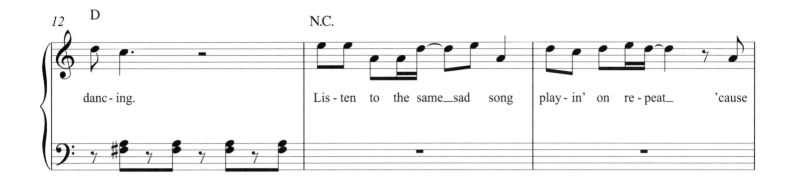
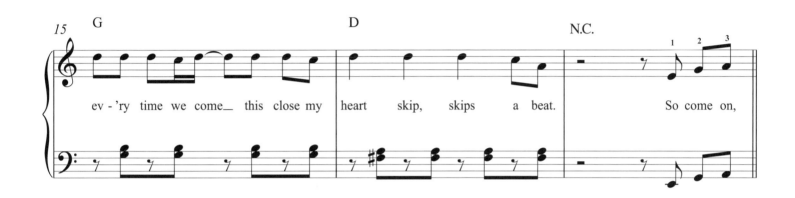
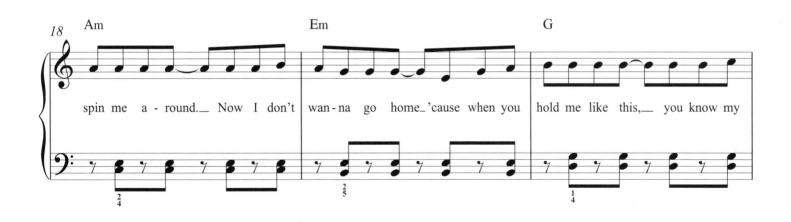

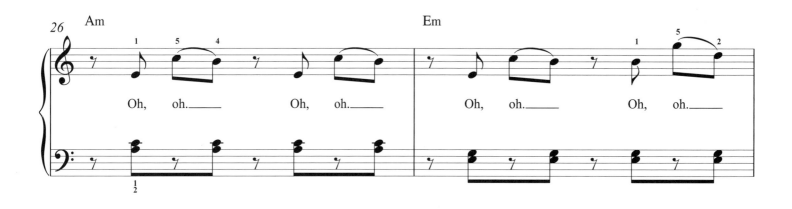
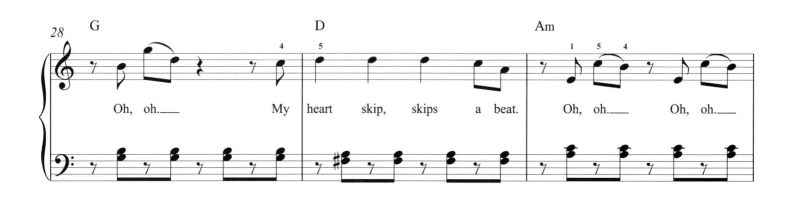

Hey You Beautiful

Words & Music by Stephen Robson, Claude Kelly & Oliver Murs

Featuring a thumping bass beat, hand claps and a choppy guitar backing, 'Hey You Beautiful' is another song that takes Olly Murs' music in a fresh new direction. With its feel-good, party vibes, the track has a similar feel to the funk-rock-pop sounds of Jamiroquai, Maroon 5 and The Noisettes, the former two of which Murs cited as key influences while writing his third album, *Right Place Right Time*.

Hints & Tips: The quavers in the left hand should be steady and even. Keep your wrists fairly light and use a 'rocking' motion to help you reach the notes.

© Copyright 2012 Studio Beast Music/Salli Isaak Music Publishing Limited/Imagem CV/Warner-Tamerlane Publishing Co.
Universal Music Publishing Limited/Imagem Music/Warner/Chappell North America Limited.
All Rights Reserved. International Copyright Secured.

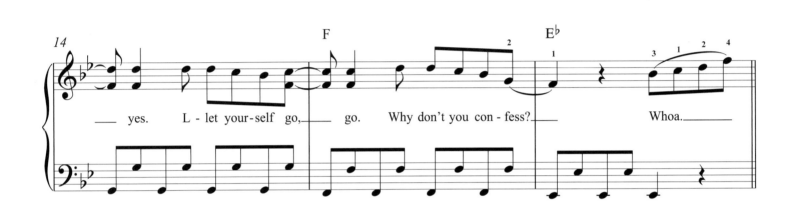
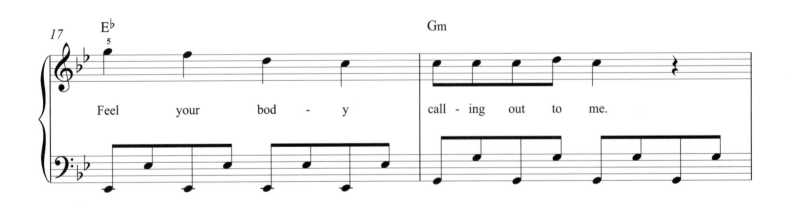
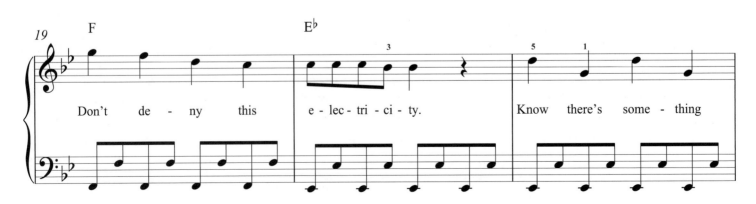

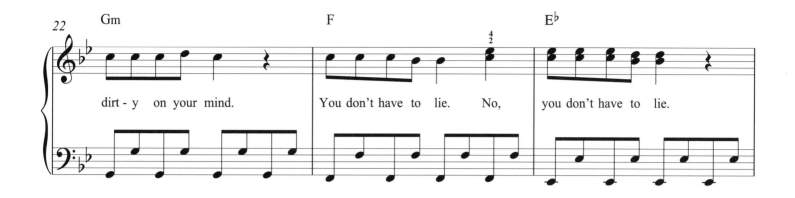

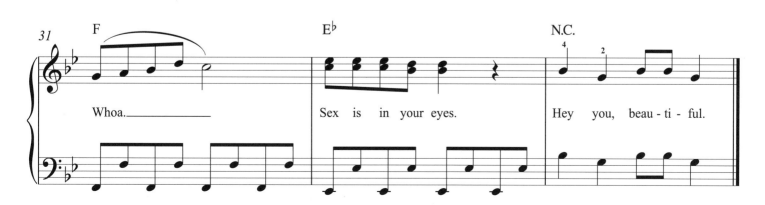

In Case You Didn't Know

**Words & Music by Stephen Robson, Claude Kelly
& Oliver Murs**

The title track from Olly Murs' second studio album, 'In Case You Didn't Know' is an upbeat ska-inspired pop hit. When writing the album Murs said that he wanted to explore new styles of music while remaining "gracious of his roots". The result was a UK Album Chart No. 1 in its first week of release, dethroning Rihanna's *Talk That Talk* – his first album to top the chart.

Hints & Tips: Pay particular attention to the fingering in this song, especially at the start where the melody moves around a lot.

I Need You Now

Words & Music by Martin Brammer, Adam Argyle & Oliver Murs

A heart-felt, piano-based number about loneliness and trying to contact an estranged love, 'I Need You Now' is another track to showcase not only Murs' vocal abilities but his talent and versatility as a songwriter. With its sparse arrangement and male-female vocal duet the song is a contrast to the more bouncy and danceable tracks on the album.

Hints & Tips: This song is in 6/8 time and has a fairly slow feel, but the melody is deceptively quick, so take your time to play through it separately before trying hands together.

© Copyright 2011 Salli Isaak Music Publishing Limited/Imagem CV/Peermusic (UK) Limited.
Universal Music Publishing Limited/Imagem Music.
All Rights Reserved. International Copyright Secured.

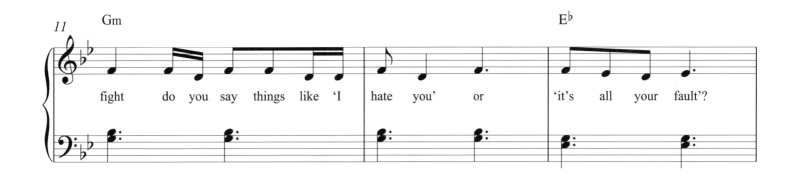
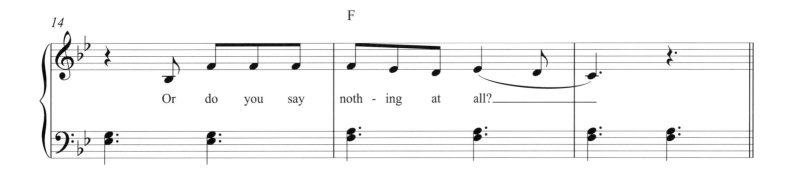
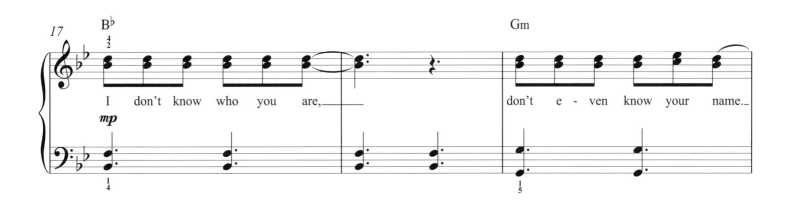

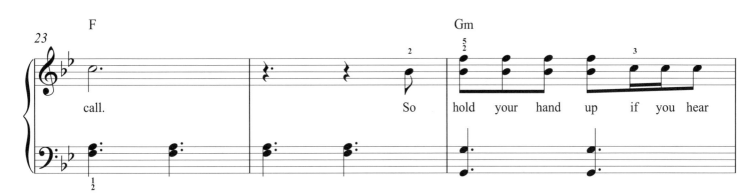

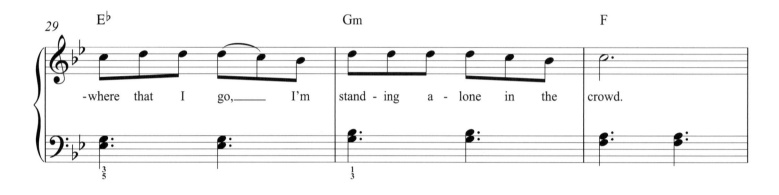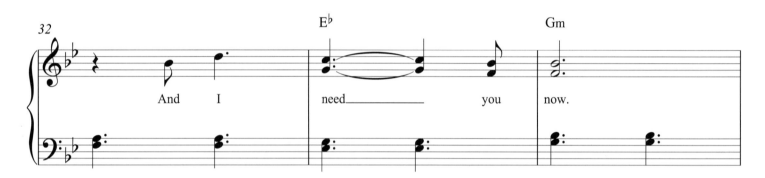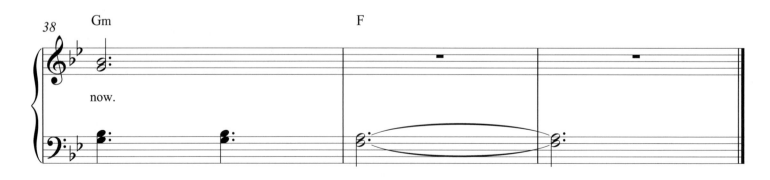

Loud & Clear

Words & Music by Claude Kelly, Charles Harmon & Oliver Murs

Co-written by Murs and American song writers and producers Chuck Harmony and Claude Kelly, 'Loud And Clear' is a strong and confident pop song driven on by a head-nodding R'n'B beat. Although not released as a single, it is one of the catchiest tracks on Murs' third album *Right Place Right Time*, with production that wouldn't sound of place at the top of the US Billboard Chart.

Hints & Tips: Look over the right hand from bar 32 before you begin, as the fingering is quite tricky. Start getting your fingers ready to change position while you're holding down the long D at the end of bar 33.

© Copyright 2012 EMI Music Publishing Limited/Universal Music Publishing Limited/Warner/Chappell North America Limited.
All Rights Reserved. International Copyright Secured.

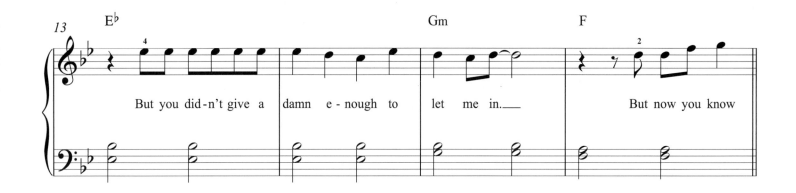
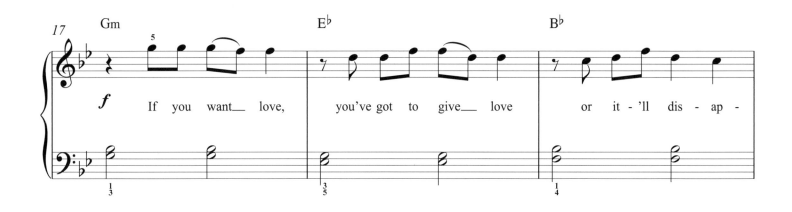

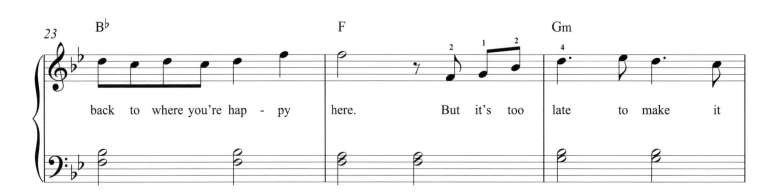

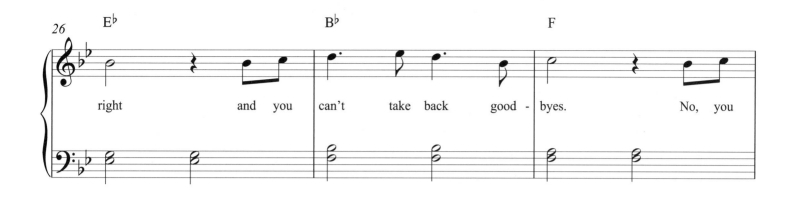
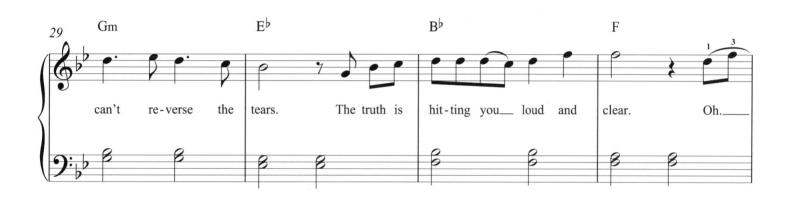
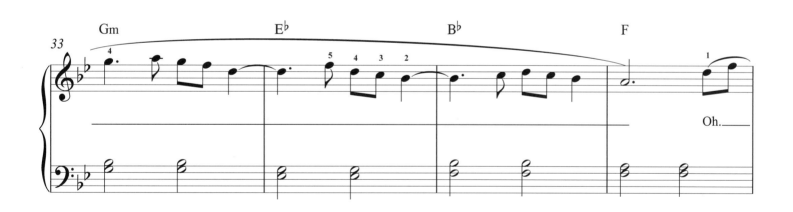
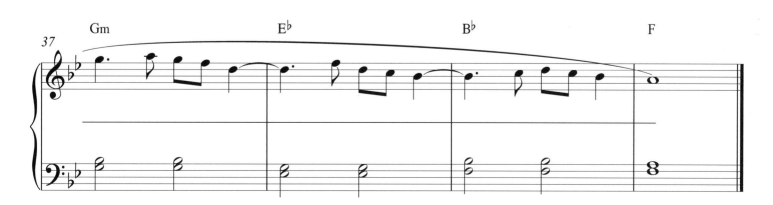

31

Oh My Goodness

Words & Music by Martin Brammer, Adam Argyle & Oliver Murs

'Oh My Goodness' tells the story of a man who falls in love a girl at first sight, inspired by Murs seeing an attractive girl whilst taking a lunch break during the recording session for his second album, *In Case You Didn't Know*. The finished song was released as the album's third and final single, becoming Murs' sixth top twenty hit in the UK.

Hints & Tips: Make the most of the dynamics in this song; while it starts off fairly soft, the chorus is marked *mezzo forte* and it should end the same volume as the beginning.

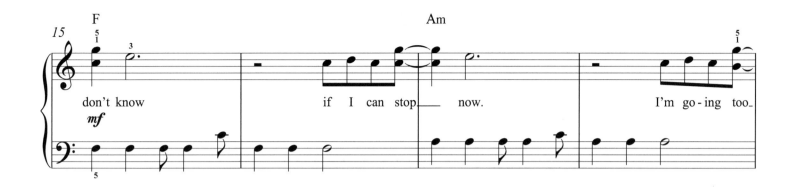
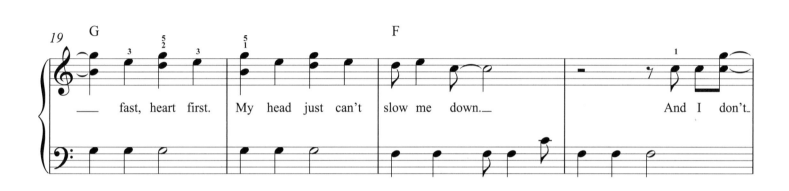
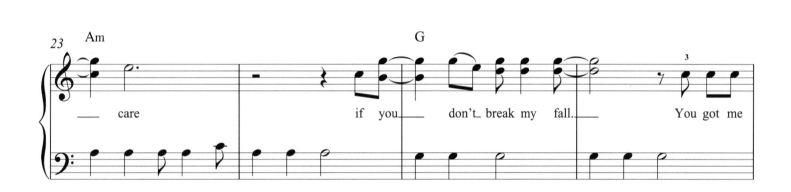
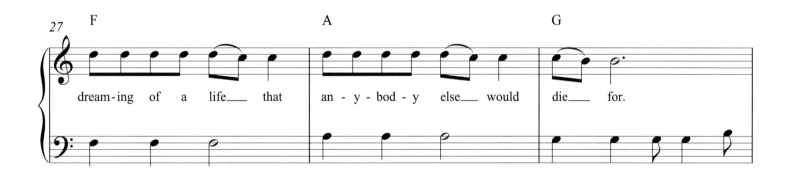
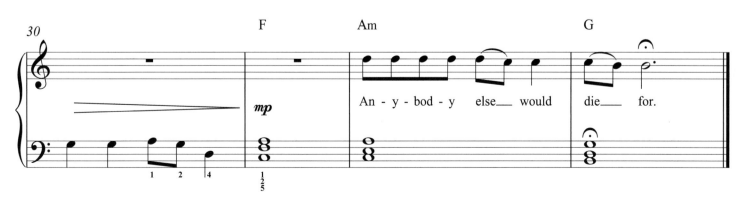

One Of These Days

**Words & Music by Andrew Frampton, Stephen Kipner,
Julian Bunetta & Oliver Murs**

Featured on Murs' third album, *Right Place Right Time*, the slower-paced 'One Of The These Days' may not have been released as a single in its own right but was prominently featured on the set list of the tour promoting the album. With its deliberate feel and growing momentum it's a song that sounds almost made for live performances.

Hints & Tips: In the first bar, you'll need to stretch down with your right hand in order to reach that bottom D, then back up again to the B. Practise this a few times until you can play it smoothly.

© Copyright 2012 Salli Isaak Music Publishing Limited/EMI April Music Inc/Andrew Frampton Music/Holy Cannoli Music.
Universal Music Publishing Limited/Stage Three Music Publishing Limited/EMI Music Publishing Limited.
All Rights Reserved. International Copyright Secured.

Please Don't Let Me Go

**Words & Music by Stephen Robson, Claude Kelly
& Oliver Murs**

A product of one of the first writing sessions for his debut album, 'Please Don't Let Me Go' helped to establish the reggae-influenced pop sound that soon became Murs' hallmark. The song became the lead single from his debut album, *Olly Murs*. Murs stated at the time that he was excited to be releasing his first single, especially since it was an original song – something he felt was important in order for him to be a success after appearing on *The X Factor*.

Hints & Tips: This song has a fairly fast feel to it, so don't let it drag. Remember to swing those quavers!

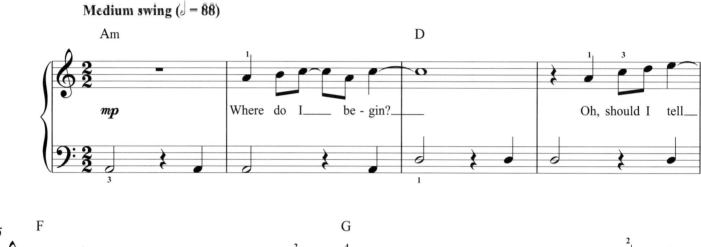

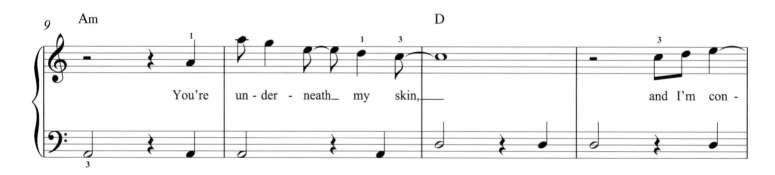

© Copyright 2010 Studio Beast Music/Salli Isaak Music Publishing Limited/Warner-Tamerlane Publishing Co.
Universal Music Publishing Limited/Warner/Chappell North America Limited/Stage Three Music Publishing Limited.
All Rights Reserved. International Copyright Secured.

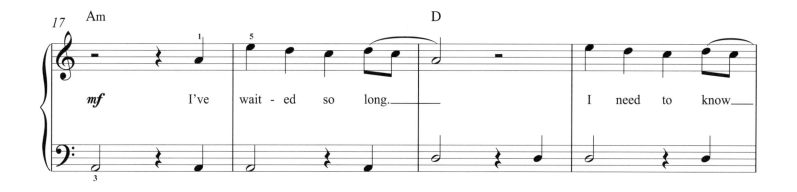
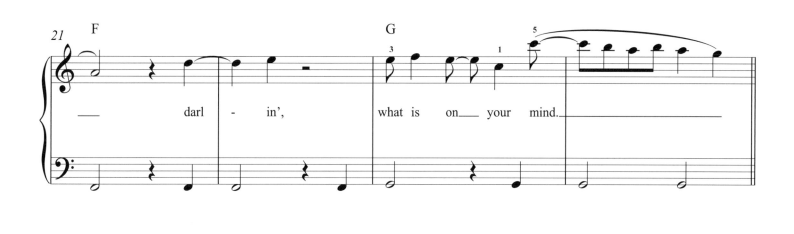
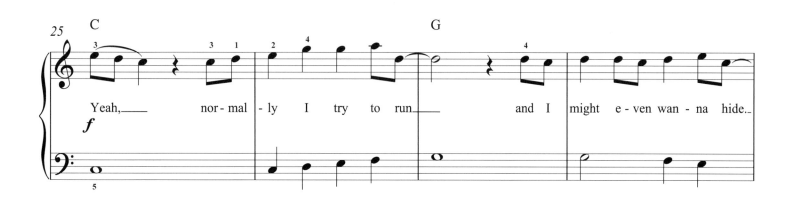
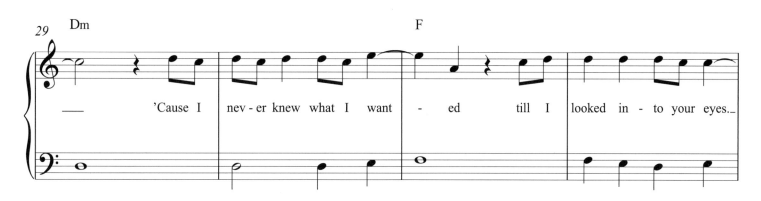

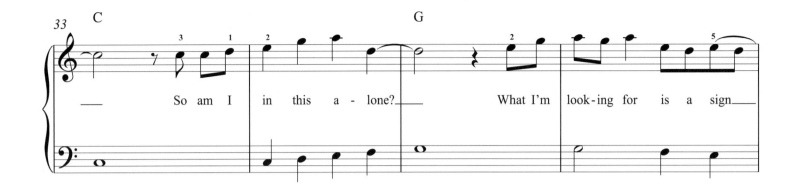

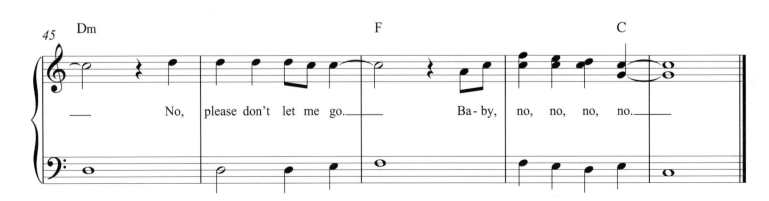

Right Place Right Time

Words & Music by Stephen Robson, Claude Kelly & Oliver Murs

'Right Place Right Time' is the title track to Olly Murs' third album. Featuring breakbeats and a prodding, rhythmic piano line that may be more familiar with electronic dance listeners, the song once again breathed fresh ideas into Murs' sound. Bursting with euphoric energy, the track was chosen as the penultimate song for the *Right Place Right Time* tour set list.

Hints & Tips: Make sure the notes of the left hand sound together throughout. It's quite a fast song, so practise it slowly at first then build up speed.

© Copyright 2013 Studio Beast Music/Salli Isaak Music Publishing Limited/Imagem CV/Warner-Tamerlane Publishing Co.
Universal Music Publishing Limited/Imagem Music/Warner/Chappell North America Limited.
All Rights Reserved. International Copyright Secured.

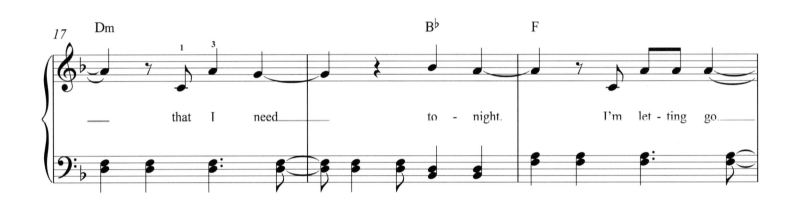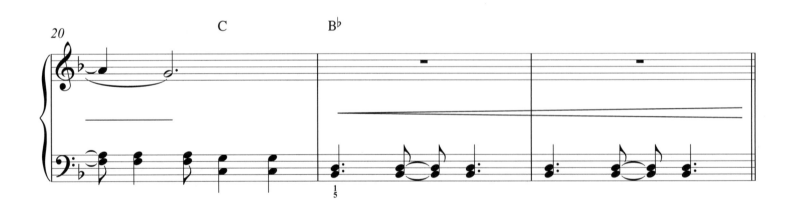

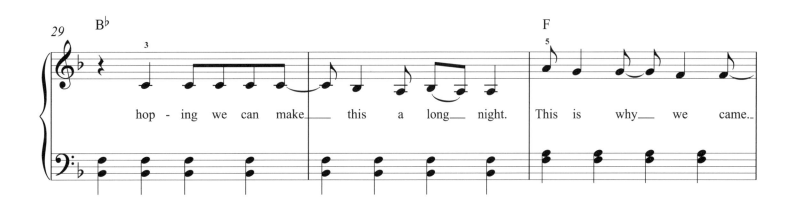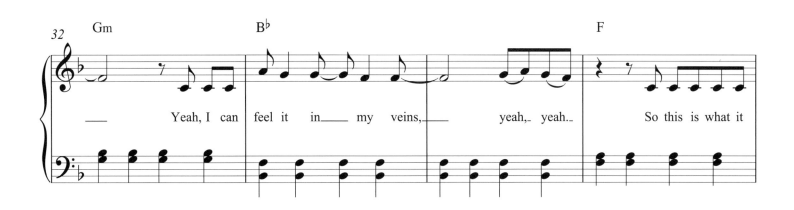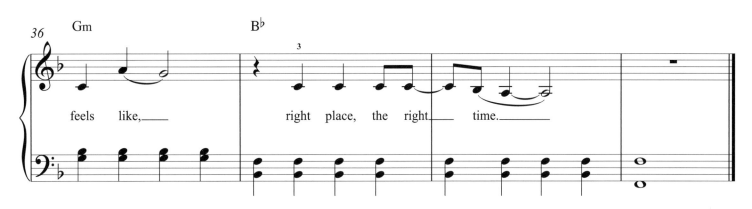

Thinking Of Me

Words & Music by Wayne Hector, Steve Robson & Oliver Murs

The second single from his debut album, this song was released in November 2010. Receiving its first airplay on BBC Radio 1 in October 2010 following an interview with Chris Moyles, the track went from strength to strength, and in December 2010 'Thinking Of Me' was featured in advert for department store chain Debenhams.

Hints & Tips: Watch out for accidentals! Look through the whole piece before you begin playing, so you know when they're coming up.

© Copyright 2010 Salli Isaak Music Publishing Limited.
Universal Music Publishing Limited/Sony/ATV Music Publishing/Stage Three Music Publishing Limited.
All Rights Reserved. International Copyright Secured.

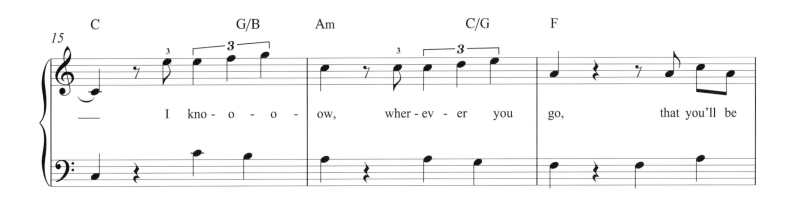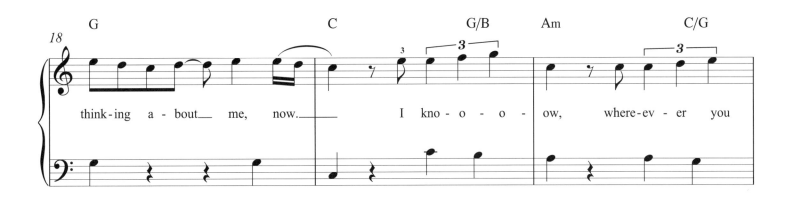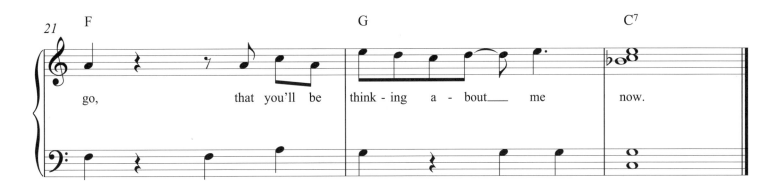

This Song Is About You

Words & Music by Stephen Robson, Claude Kelly & Oliver Murs

A confessional track recounting Olly Murs' struggles with a problematic relationship, 'This Song Is About You' talks of regret about being with someone holding the singer back, and the sense of relief, release and freedom after they've split up and the catharsis of the song has helped to heal his wounds.

Hints & Tips: This is quite a slow song, but the melody uses a lots of semiquavers so count carefully. Note that the left hand plays the same 2-bar chord pattern throughout.

© Copyright 2011 Studio Beast Music/Salli Isaak Music Publishing Limited/Imagem CV/Warner-Tamerlane Publishing Co.
Universal Music Publishing Limited/Imagem Music/Warner/Chappell North America Limited.
All Rights Reserved. International Copyright Secured.

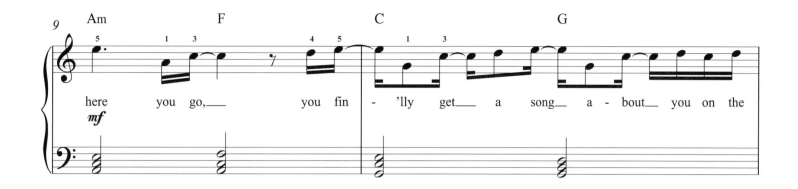
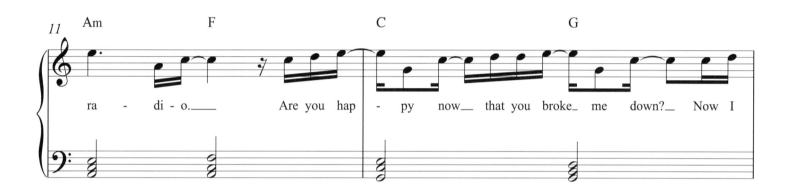
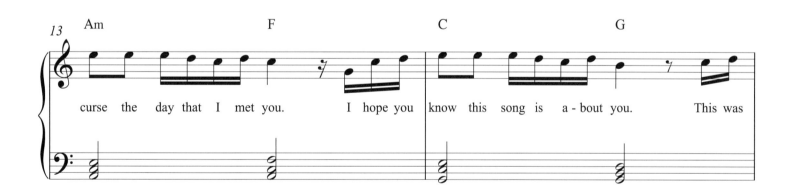
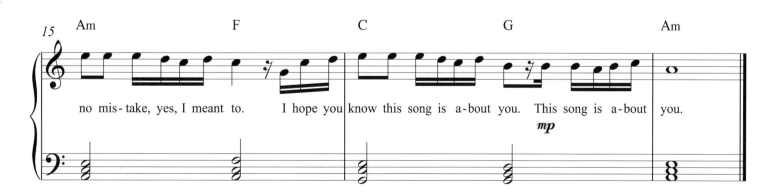

Troublemaker

Words & Music by Stephen Robson, Claude Kelly, Flo Rida & Oliver Murs

Written by Murs, Claude Kelly and Steve Robson, this is a song about that special girl with a wild side that you can't shake off – she might not be good for you but you can't help yourself. The track also features American rapper Flo Rida, who agreed to appear on the song after hearing the demo, telling ITV's *Daybreak*: "I know a hit record when I hear it." 'Troublemaker' was a UK No. 1 and peaked at 25 on the US Billboard Singles Chart.

Hints & Tips: Play through this hands separately to begin with, as the left hand is quite tricky, with lots of syncopation.

© Copyright 2012 Studio Beast Music/Salli Isaak Music Publishing Limited/Sony/ATV Tunes LLC/Warner-Tamerlane Publishing Co/Imagem CV.
Universal Music Publishing Limited/Sony/ATV Music Publishing/Imagem Music/Warner/Chappell North America Limited.
All Rights Reserved. International Copyright Secured.

Bringing you the words and the music

All the latest music in print... rock & pop plus jazz, blues, country, classical and the best in West End show scores.

- Books to match your favourite CDs.

- Book-and-CD titles with high quality backing tracks for you to play along to. Now you can play guitar or piano with your favourite artist... or simply sing along!

- Audition songbooks with CD backing tracks for both male and female singers for all those with stars in their eyes.

- Can't read music? No problem, you can still play all the hits with our wide range of chord songbooks.

- Check out our range of instrumental tutorial titles, taking you from novice to expert in no time at all!

- Musical show scores include *The Phantom Of The Opera*, *Les Misérables*, *Mamma Mia* and many more hit productions.

- DVD master classes featuring the techniques of top artists.

Visit your local music shop or, in case of difficulty, contact the Marketing Department, Music Sales Limited, Newmarket Road, Bury St Edmunds, Suffolk, IP33 3YB, UK
marketing@musicsales.co.uk